Let's Celebrate with More HALLOWEEN ORIGAMI

By Ruth Owen

Enslow PUBLISHING

Published in 2022 by Enslow Publishing, LLC
29 East 21st Street
New York, NY 10010

Copyright © 2022 Enslow Publishing, LLC
All rights reserved.

Produced for Rosen by Ruth Owen Books
Designer: Emma Randall
Photos courtesy of Ruth Owen Books and Shutterstock

Cataloging-in-Publication Data

Names: Owen, Ruth.
Title: Let's celebrate with more Halloween origami / Ruth Owen.
Description: New York : Enslow Publishing, 2022. | Series: Let's celebrate with origami | Includes glossary and index.
Identifiers: ISBN 9781978526594 (pbk.) | ISBN 9781978526617 (library bound) | ISBN 9781978526600 (6 pack) | ISBN 9781978526624 (ebook)
Subjects: LCSH: Origami--Juvenile literature. | Halloween decorations--Juvenile literature.
Classification: LCC TT870.O946 2022 | DDC 736'.982--dc23

All rights reserved. No part of this book may be reproduced in any form without permission in writing from the publisher, except by a reviewer.

Manufactured in the United States of America

CPSIA compliance information: Batch #CWENS22: For further information contact Enslow Publishing, New York, New York at 1-800-398-2504

Find us on

Contents

Creepy Origami 4

Origami Tips 6

A Flying Witch 8

A Warty Toad 12

Fold a Vampire 16

A Scary Skull 20

Jack-o'-Lantern Lights 24

Spooky Spider 28

Glossary, Index, Websites 32

Creepy Origami

Folding paper to create models is called **origami**. This craft is a great way to make decorations for Halloween, such as vampire faces, scary skulls, a spooky spider, and jack-o'-lanterns.

The word origami comes from the Japanese language. In Japanese, "ori" means folding, and "kami" means paper. No one knows how origami got started, but it's been popular for centuries, especially in Japan.

Whether you're an origami beginner or have tried making paper **sculptures** before, this book has a project for you. Just follow the step-by-step instructions and your origami Halloween will soon be taking shape!

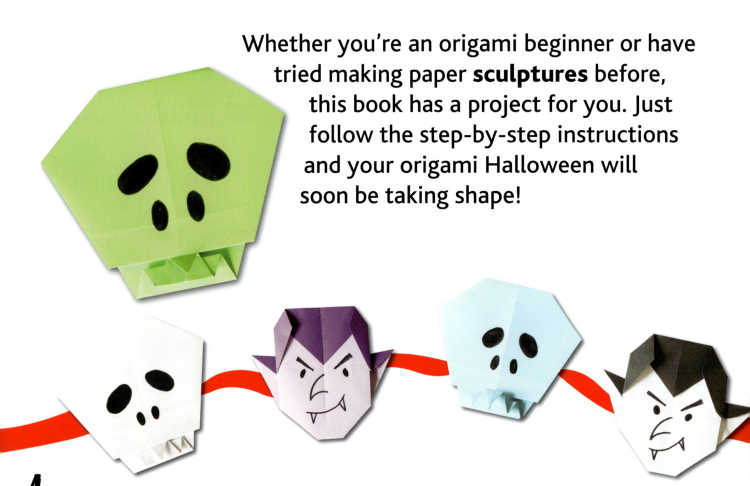

5

Origami Tips

Follow these tips for successful folding and origami model making.

Tip 1
Read all the instructions carefully and look at the pictures. Make sure you understand what's required before you begin a fold. Don't rush; be patient. Work slowly and carefully.

Tip 2
Folding a piece of paper sounds easy, but it can be tricky to get neat, accurate folds. The more you practice, the easier it becomes.

Tip 3
If an instruction says "crease," make the crease as flat as possible. The flatter the creases, the better the model. You can make a sharp crease by running a plastic ruler along the edge of the paper.

Tip 4
Sometimes, at first, your models may look a little crumpled. Don't give up! The more models you make, the better you will get at folding and creasing.

When it comes to origami, practice makes perfect!

The colorful ball, swan, and bony hands on this page were made by experienced origami model makers. They look complicated, but with practice, you could soon be making impressive paper sculptures like these!

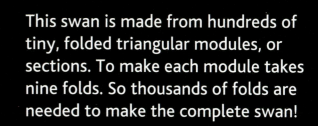

This swan is made from hundreds of tiny, folded triangular modules, or sections. To make each module takes nine folds. So thousands of folds are needed to make the complete swan!

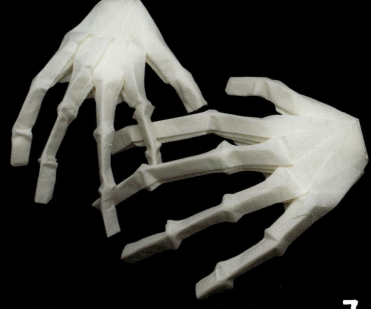

A Flying Witch

In old **folklore**, it's said that witches can fly by riding on magical broomsticks. These scary (and sometimes ugly) old women can also use their **supernatural** powers to cast spells. Often, their spells are said to cause harm to people—especially children!

To make an origami witch and broomstick, you will need:

- A sheet of origami paper that's black on one side and white on the other
- Glue
- Scissors
- A sheet of paper in your color choice to make the broomstick (the same size as the piece used to make the witch)

STEP 1:
Place the paper black side down. Fold in half, crease, and unfold.

STEP 2:
Fold in the two sides of the model so that they meet at the center crease and form a kite shape. Crease well.

STEP 3:
Fold down the top point to meet the bottom point, crease, and unfold.

STEP 4:
Fold up the bottom point, and crease.

STEP 5:
Now fold down the top point to meet the crease you made in Step 3, crease, and unfold.

STEP 6:
Now fold back the two flaps in the center of the model, and crease.

STEP 7:
Fold the model in half, and crease the right-hand edge well.

STEP 8:
Fold down the top point of the model along the dotted line, crease hard, and unfold.

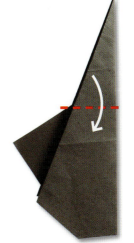

STEP 9:

Fold down the top point again at an angle along the dotted line. The fold should cross diagonally between the creases you made in Step 5 and Step 8. Crease hard, and unfold.

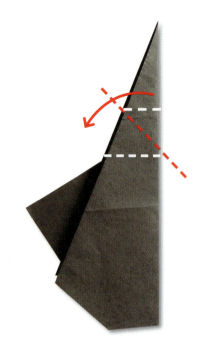

Now hold the model with your thumb and forefinger just below the crease you made in Step 8. Open out the top point of the model, and using the crease you made in Step 8 and the diagonal crease you've just made, gently squash and fold down the top point so it lies flat against the model.

STEP 10:

Now fold the point of the hat back toward the right-hand side. You will see a tiny white triangle appear that is the witch's face. Then fold back the brim of the hat to reveal more of the witch's face.

STEP 11:
To make the broomstick, cut a sheet of paper in half. Take one half and then fold it in half, and crease.

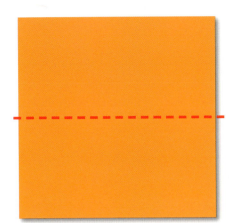

STEP 12:
Unfold the crease you just made. Now fold the top section of the paper in half to meet the center, and crease. Repeat on the bottom.

STEP 13:
Fold in the right-hand side of the model along the dotted line, and crease. Then fold it back again to create a small pleat.

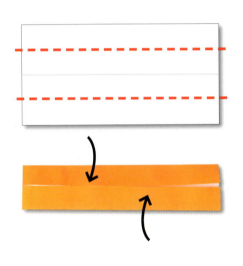

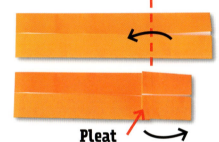

Pleat

STEP 14:
Fold down the top half of the model along the dotted line, and crease hard. Then gently open out the top right-hand edge of the model to create the twiggy end of the broom.

STEP 15:
Slot the witch onto the broomstick. You can use a little glue to hold her in place.

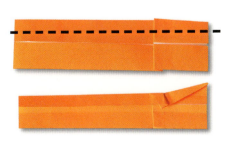

Repeat on the bottom of the model.

11

A Warty Toad

Old stories say that witches often lived with an animal such as a black dog, an owl, a black cat, or a toad. Why? These animal companions were known as familiars. They had supernatural powers of their own and helped the witch with her magical spells.

Witches didn't only have toads as familiars. They sometimes used the animals in their magical brews. A poor toad might be dropped into a witch's pot as an ingredient as she stirred up a wicked potion!

In this next project, you can make a toad. Choose some green paper and remember to draw some warty lumps and bumps on your toad!

To make an origami toad, you will need:

One sheet of green origami paper

Scissors

Colored pens

(Origami paper is sometimes colored on both sides or white on one side.)

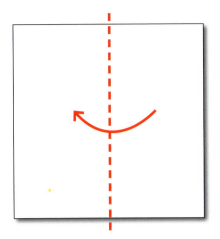

STEP 1:
Place the paper colored side down, fold in half, and crease.

STEP 2:
Fold over the top left-hand corner of the model, crease, and then unfold. Repeat on the top right-hand corner.

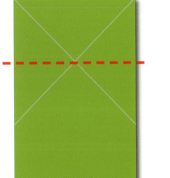

STEP 3:
Now fold over the top of the model. You should fold at the place where the creases you made in step 2 meet. Then unfold.

STEP 4:
Take hold of the two sides of the model and begin to squash them into the center. As you do this, the creases you've made will make the top of the model collapse into a triangle.

13

STEP 5:

To make the toad's front legs, fold up the two bottom points of the triangle along the dotted lines, and crease hard.

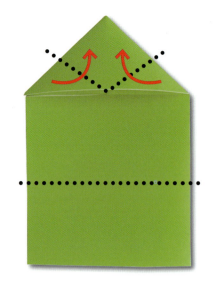

Then fold up the bottom half of the model, and crease.

STEP 6:

Now fold in the sides of the model so that they meet in the center. Crease hard.

STEP 7:

Fold up the bottom of the model, and crease hard. Now open out the bottom of the model to make a pocket. Squash down and flatten the pocket against the model.

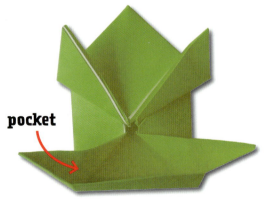

pocket

flattened pocket

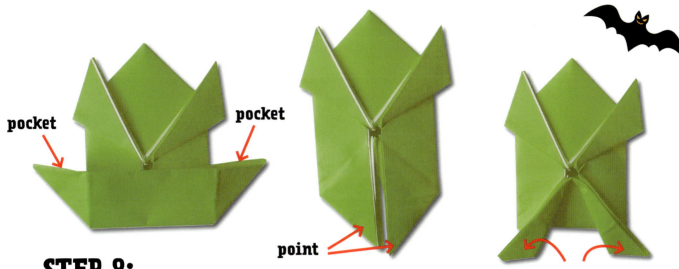

STEP 8:
Next, open out one of the side pockets at the bottom of the model. Then squash and flatten it down to create a point. Repeat on the other side.

Then fold back each point to create the toads's back legs.

STEP 9:
Fold up the bottom of the model, and crease hard. Then fold it back down again, making a small pleat.

STEP 10:
Flip the model over and your toad is complete. If you wish, draw colorful warty lumps on your toad.

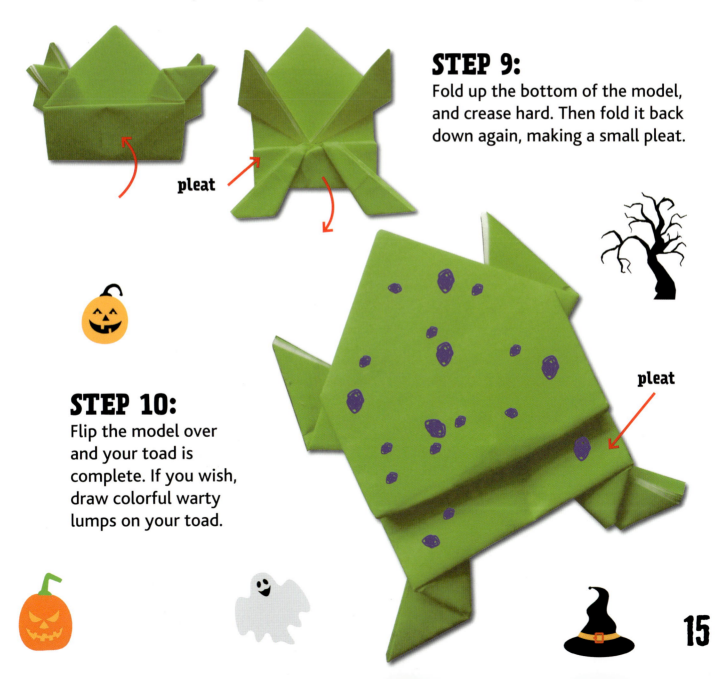

15

Fold a Vampire

Would you like a bloodsucking undead creature to decorate your home at Halloween? Then this vampire model is the perfect project for you. Vampires are **corpses** that have returned from the dead to drink the blood of the living.

Many vampire stories say that a vampire's skin will burn if exposed to sunlight. So vampires sleep by day in their coffins or tombs. At night, they wake up to hunt and feed. It is said that some vampires can fly, while others have the strength of 20 men!

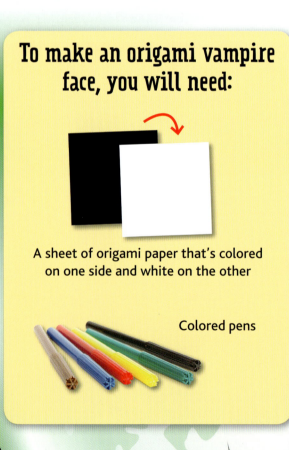

To make an origami vampire face, you will need:

A sheet of origami paper that's colored on one side and white on the other

Colored pens

STEP 1:
Place the paper colored side down. Fold in half, crease, and unfold.

STEP 2:
Fold the top corner of the model down to meet the center, and crease.

STEP 3:
Fold in the two sides of the model along the dotted lines, and crease.

STEP 4:
Turn the model over. Fold in the two sides of the model so that they meet at the center crease, and crease.

STEP 5:
To make the vampire's ears, fold back the two points that are now in the center of the model, and crease.

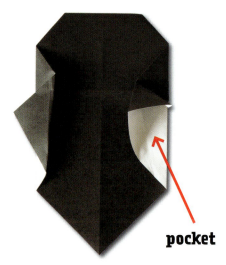

pocket

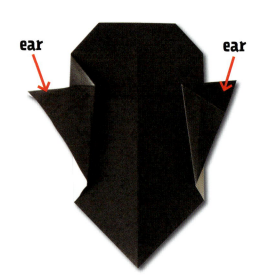

ear   ear

Open out the fold you've just made on the right-hand side to form a pocket. Gently squash the pocket flat. Repeat on the left-hand side.

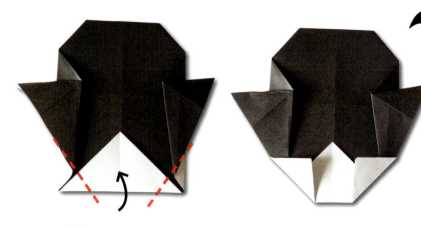

STEP 6:

To make the vampire's chin, fold up the bottom point of the model, and crease.

Fold in the two bottom corners of the model along the dotted lines, and crease hard.

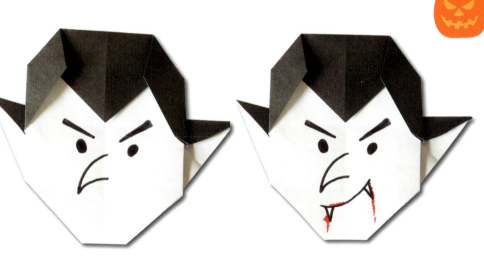

STEP 7:

Turn the model over. Draw on eyebrows, eyes, and a pointed nose.

Then draw your vampire's mouth and fangs. You can draw on blood, too!

If you wish, you can make a vampire face in other colors. As long as the paper has one dark side and one light side, the vampire design will work.

19

A Scary Skull

Using squares of white or colored paper, you can make these scary skulls with big, black, hollow eyes and jagged teeth.

Skeletons and rattling bones are a favorite spooky decoration at Halloween, so try making lots of skulls and then string them together. You can add some vampire faces, too, and create your own unique and ghoulish bunting.

Let's get folding and have fun!

To make origami skulls, you will need:

Squares of white paper, or paper in your choice of colors

A ruler and pencil

A black marker

STEP 1:
Fold a square of paper in half, crease, and unfold.

STEP 2:
Fold in the two sides of the model so that they meet at the center crease and form a kite shape. Crease well.

STEP 3:
Fold down the top point of the model, and crease.

STEP 4:
Now fold up the bottom point of the model, and crease. Then fold back down again, creating a small pleat.

pleat

STEP 5:
Now turn the model over. Using the ruler, measure the bottom point of the model so that you can divide it into five equal sections. Use a pencil to lightly mark the divisions.

22

STEP 6:

Now fold up the bottom of the model along the highest division mark that you've made. Crease hard. Then fold the bottom of the model back down again along the next division mark.

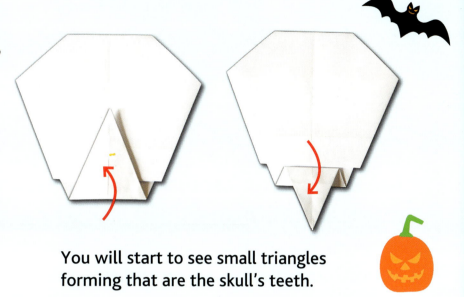

You will start to see small triangles forming that are the skull's teeth.

Fold the bottom of the model back up again, and crease hard. Finally, fold down the remaining small point to complete the skull's mouthful of teeth.

STEP 7:

Using a marker, draw on the skull's nostrils and big, black, hollow eyes.

String together skulls and vampire faces to make this cool Halloween undead decoration!

23

Jack-o'-Lantern Lights

The **tradition** of carving lanterns with scary faces from vegetables—such as potatoes, turnips, and pumpkins—has been around for centuries. It first began in Ireland with an old **myth** about a man named Jack who played tricks on the devil.

When Jack died, God would not let him into heaven. The devil rejected him too. So Jack walked the earth as a ghost—forever! He carried a lantern carved from a turnip, and was known as "Jack of the lantern."

This Halloween, you can create some pumpkin lights by making origami pumpkins and then slotting them onto the bulbs of some Christmas lights.

To make pumpkin lights, you will need:

Sheets of origami paper in orange, yellow, or red

A string of Christmas lights if you wish to make pumpkin lights

A black marker

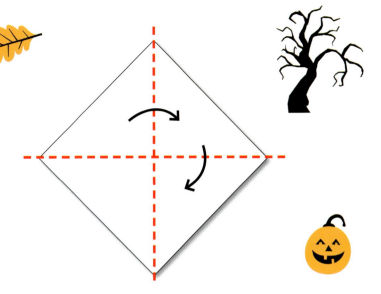

STEP 1:

Place the paper colored side down. Fold in half from side to side, crease, and unfold. Then fold down from top to bottom, crease, and unfold.

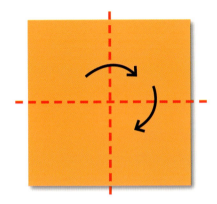

Turn the paper over. Fold in half from side to side, crease, and unfold. Then fold down from top to bottom, crease, and unfold.

STEP 2:

Place the paper colored side down. Using the creases you've just made, collapse and fold up the paper to form a flattened triangle by bringing A in to meet B, point C down to meet point D, and point E down to meet point F.

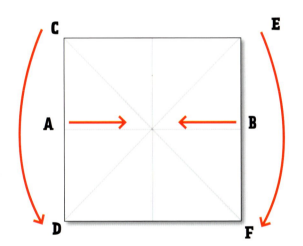

As you collapse and fold up the paper, it should look like this.

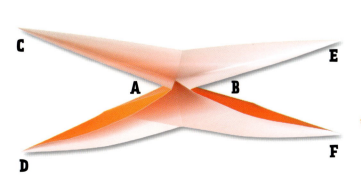

flattened triangle

25

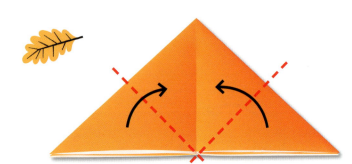

STEP 3:
Fold in the two side points of the triangle along the dotted lines, working with only the top layer of paper. Crease hard.

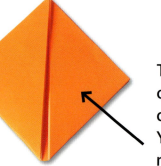

Turn the model over and repeat on the other side. Your model should now look like this.

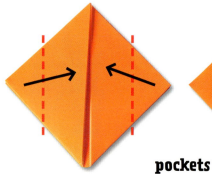

STEP 4:
Working with just the top layer of paper again, fold in the two side points to meet the center crease, and crease hard. Turn the model over, and repeat on the other side.

You will see that this has formed two small pockets on each side of the model.

STEP 5:
Fold down the two top points of the model, and crease hard.

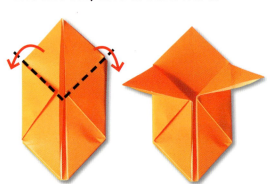

Fold the two points back in to create two small triangles.

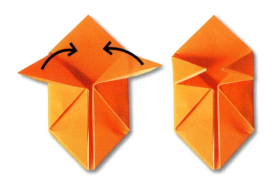

26

STEP 6:

Now take the right-hand small triangle and tuck it into the pocket you made in Step 4. Repeat on the left-hand side.

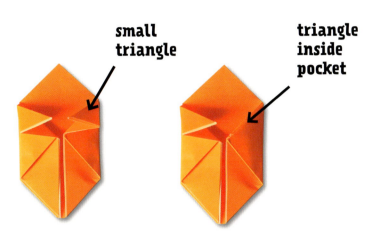

Then turn the model over and repeat on the other side.

STEP 7:

Now open out the model where there is a flat side, and draw on a face. Repeat on the other flat side.

STEP 8:

At one end of your model, you will find a little opening. Blow hard into the opening and your pumpkin will inflate!

STEP 9:

Make lots of pumpkins. Ask an adult to help you carefully slip the open end of each pumpkin over a bulb on your string of Christmas lights.

27

Spooky Spider

This model has lots of steps, but work carefully and slowly, and you will soon see a fantastic origami spider emerge from a square of paper. This is a complicated project, but it's worth it! After all, it won't be Halloween unless there are some spooky black spiders dangling in dark corners.

To make an origami spider, you will need:

One sheet of origami paper that's black or brown

Scissors

STEP 1:
Place the paper white side down. Fold in half along the dotted lines, crease, and unfold.

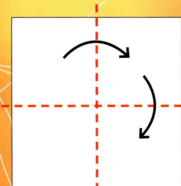

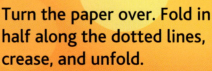

Turn the paper over. Fold in half along the dotted lines, crease, and unfold.

28

STEP 2:

Place the paper white side down. When viewed from above, it should now look like this.

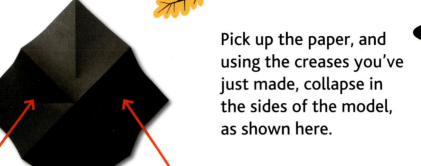

Pick up the paper, and using the creases you've just made, collapse in the sides of the model, as shown here.

Collapse in here.

Collapse in here.

Squash down.

STEP 3:

Squash down on the model to form a square.

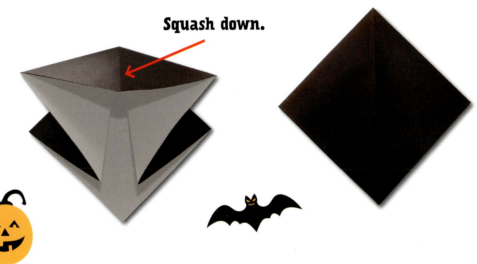

STEP 4:

Take hold of the right-hand side point of the square (just the top layer of paper). Lift it up, open it out slightly, and then gently squash it flat to form an upside-down kite shape.

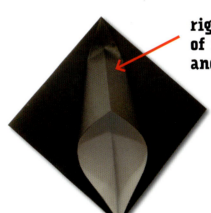

right-hand point of model, lifted and opened out

upside-down kite shape

Now, opening and closing each of the other three sides of your model in turns, repeat what you've just done on the other three points until your model looks like this.

29

STEP 5:

Next, working with just one diamond and the top layer of paper, fold each of the bottom edges into the center of the model, crease hard, and unfold.

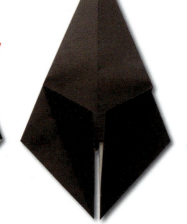
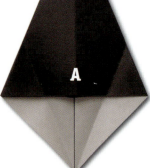

Now gently lift up the section marked A to form a pocket. Then, using the creases you've just made, squash and flatten the pocket to create a small kite shape.

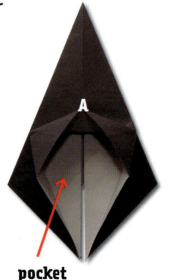

pocket

small kite shape

Again, move around your model, repeating everything you've done in step 5 three more times until your model looks like this.

STEP 6:

Now open up your model at a flat section that contains no kite shape. Working with just the top layer of paper, fold the two sides into the center crease along the dotted lines, and crease hard. Now repeat on the model's other three flat sections.

flat section with no kite shape

Your model should look like this.

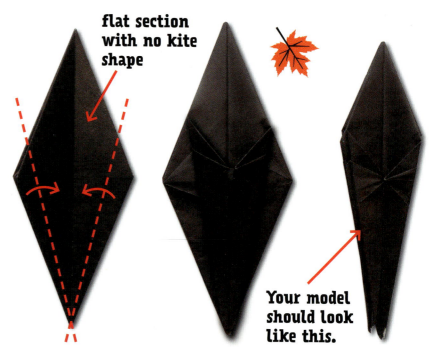

Cut up the center of each long point.

two points (or legs) created by cutting

STEP 7:
Your model will now have four long, pointed sections. Carefully cut up the center of each point to create eight points, or legs.

Open up the model to a section that contains a small kite shape, and begin folding the legs out to the side.

To round off the spider's body, you can fold the end point under.

Fold the point of the body under here.

Open out a section with a kite shape.

STEP 8:
Fold some of the legs forward and some backward to create a realistic shape for your origami spider.

Glossary

corpses
Dead bodies. This word is usually used in relation to humans.

folklore
Stories and beliefs that are common to a certain group or culture. Folklore is often passed from generation to generation by word of mouth.

myth
A story told to explain something in nature or society, usually including supernatural beings or events.

origami
The art of folding paper into decorative shapes or objects.

sculptures
Works of art that have a shape to them, such as statues or carved objects, and may be made of wood, stone, metal, plaster, or even paper.

supernatural
Something that does not follow the laws of nature and cannot be explained by science.

tradition
A custom, belief, or practice that has existed for a long time and has been passed on from one generation to the next.

Index

F
familiars, 12
flying witch origami model, 8–9, 10–11

J
jack-o'-lantern light model, 24–25, 26–27
jack-o'-lanterns, 4, 24
Japan, 4

O
origami (general), 4, 6–7

S
skull origami model, 20–21, 22–23
skulls, 5, 20
spiders, 4, 28
spooky spider origami model, 28–29, 30–31

T
toad origami model, 12–13, 14–15
toads, 12

V
vampire origami model, 16–17, 18–19
vampires, 4, 16

W
witches, 8, 12

Websites

www.marthastewart.com/275085/kids-halloween-crafts
www.origami-resource-center.com/halloween-origami.html
www.thesprucecrafts.com/pumpkin-carving-ideas-for-kids-4153104

Publisher's note to educators and parents: Our editors have carefully reviewed these websites to ensure that they are suitable for students. Many websites change frequently, however, and we cannot guarantee that a site's future contents will continue to meet our high standards of quality and educational value. Be advised that students should be closely supervised whenever they access the internet.